# That's not my...
## colouring book
### Farm

This book belongs to...

_____

That's not my hen.

That's my _ _ _.

That's not my cow.

That's my — — —

That's not my pig.

That's my _ _ _ !

That's not my farmhouse.

That's my _ _ _ _ _ _ _.

That's not my
scarecrow.

That's my

- - - - - - - - - - - - - - - - - - - - - - .

That's not my sheep.

That's my _ _ _ _ _ _ .

That's not my goat.

That's my _____.

That's not my tractor.

That's my _____.

That's not my cat.

That's my _ _ _ _.

That's not my
cockerel.

That's my

_____

That's not my sheepdog.

That's my _ _ _ _ _ _ _.

That's not my horse.

That's my _ _ _ _ _ _

That's not my duck.

That's my _ _ _ _ _ _ _ .

That's not my barn.

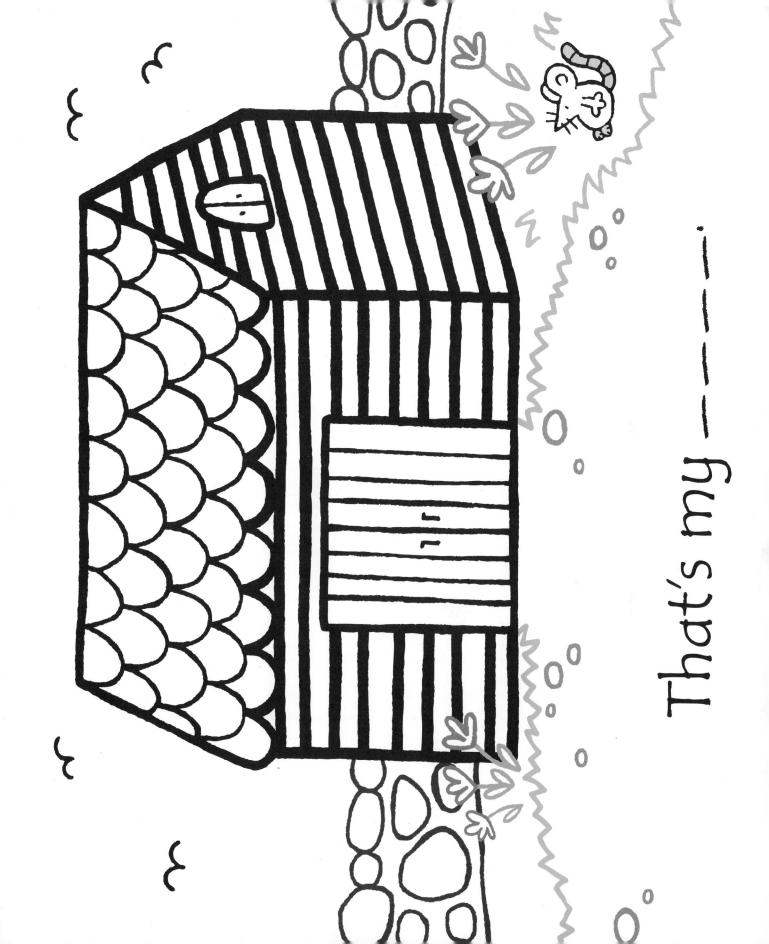

That's my ___ ___.

oink oink

pig

cock-a-doodle-doo!

farmhouse

cockerel

woof woof

sheepdog

moo

cow

baa

sheep

bleat

goat

quack
quack

duck

scarecrow